I WAS A TEENAGE PROFESSIONAL WRESTLER

 A Richard Jackson Book

I WAS A TEENAGE PROFESSIONAL WRESTLER

Ted Lewin

*Illustrated with photographs &
sketches and paintings by
the author*

Orchard Books / New York

Note: Many of the photographs reproduced in this book are forty
years old. Credit has been given to sources and photographers
whenever possible, but several pictures are publicity shots that
wrestlers handed out as souvenirs to fans at matches, and these
rarely cite a photographer's name. Photographs on pages ii, 58, 64,
66–67, 77, 86, 87, 88, 102, 109, 110, 118, 119, 120, 121, and 124
were taken by the author.

Orchard Books, 95 Madison Avenue, New York, NY 10016

Manufactured in the United States of America
The text of this book is set in 12 point Meridien.
10   9   8   7   6   5   4   3   2

Library of Congress Cataloging-in-Publication Data
Lewin, Ted. I was a teenage professional wrestler / by Ted Lewin ;
illustrated with photographs & sketches and paintings by the author.
p.   cm.   "A Richard Jackson book."
Summary: The author-illustrator describes his early days supporting
himself as a professional wrestler.
ISBN 0-531-05477-2   ISBN 0-531-08627-5 (lib. bdg.)
1. Lewin, Ted—Juvenile literature.   2. Wrestlers—United States—
Biography—Juvenile literature.   3. Illustrators—United States—
Biography—Juvenile literature.   [1. Lewin, Ted.   2. Wrestlers.
3. Illustrators.   4. Authors, American.]   I. Title.
GV1196.L48A3   1993   796.8'12'092—dc20   [B]   92-31523

Frontispiece: Laurel Garden, Newark, New Jersey
Title page: 1952 photo of me, taken by a fan in Ohio

For my mother and father, whom
I loved dearly.

And for Ed Grimm, for his help and
guidance over the years.

And for Richard Jackson, for seeing the
way it should be.

Contents

PART TWO

The Lewin Brothers—Ted, Mark, and Donn, left to right—ready for a six-man tag team match, Washington, D.C.

Preface

In the summer of 1952, at age seventeen, I became a professional wrestler. The work paid my way through art school and, for fifteen years, helped support me until I was able to make a living as a full-time illustrator and writer.

My two brothers, Donn and Mark, were also professional wrestlers, as was my brother-in-law, Dangerous Danny McShain, the junior heavyweight champion of the world from 1951 to 1954.

It was a great life, crowded with unforgettable characters: college men, working men with bleached hair, ugly men and men who could have been movie stars, huge fat men in outrageous costumes, men from all over the world. (In many states, laws prohibited women from wrestling, and in some they still do.)

Wrestlers radiate a kind of bizarre charm, a combination of carny and talk-show host. They make you look sideways at what they're saying (with a sincere face), yet you want to believe. After all, they've been around.

Around where? Around the country? The world? Sure, but mainly around one another. They draw on one another, need one another. The audience—whom the wrestlers call the "marks"—they need in a different way. The marks pay to get in and watch. And after all, what's the game for without somebody watching?

Wrestlers are vagabonds. They travel thousands of miles, work out, lift weights, run, keep in shape—all for the ten or twenty minutes where they really live, where they are lost in the fantasies of a crowd. A few months booked here, a few months booked there—always moving on, trying out new faces (sometimes a new face is an old one covered with a mask). They move on and on with or without family. Their lives revolve around the business, around one another. The wrestling way of life is infectious: it gets inside your head. While you're in it, you think like a wrestler, and *no one* but a wrestler thinks like one.

PART ONE

*Sun porch and backyard of our house in Buffalo, New York,
where it all began*

Young Fans

My father used to take my brother Mark and me to wrestling matches when we were little kids in Upstate New York. Our older brother, Donn, had joined the marines at sixteen—my parents signed for him—and was fighting World War II in the Pacific.

By the time Mark was twelve and I was fourteen, we were allowed to go to Friday-night wrestling on our own. Matches were held in the winter, and all through those tough months Mark and I would take the downtown bus to the end of the line at Buffalo's Memorial Auditorium, a big cavern of a place that sat about fourteen thousand. Snow, sleet—nothing could keep us away.

We'd get a program, load up on popcorn, and find our seats at ringside. Then out they'd come, some of the all-time greats: Ed Don George versus Jim ("Goon") Henry; Frank Sexton versus Ski Hi Lee; Wee Willie Davis versus the French Angel; Whipper Billy Watson versus Pat Flannagan. We'd be spellbound, shoving the popcorn in as fast as we could.

We booed when everyone else did, cheered when everyone else cheered. "Make him break," we'd yell. "He's choking him." "He's using the ropes." We studied every move—every go-behind and takedown. We watched wrestlers strut and fly through the air, burning the impressions into our brains. We marveled at the noises they made, then imitated them on the way home.

When we got there, bursting with excitement, my mother and father would be waiting for us, propped up in bed, reading detective magazines.

"You should have seen the dropkicks." . . . "You know what Jim Goon did to Ed Don George?" . . . "Then Ed Don, he . . ."

Our parents would laugh and exchange glances.

"They're all a bunch of fakers," my father would say, just to bug us.

"You don't understand," we'd answer. "Wait. We'll show you." Then we'd race into the large sun porch just off their bedroom so they could watch without getting up. It was cold in that glass space after dark, but we'd strip down to our undershorts anyhow, pull the four-by-six-foot mat we kept there into the middle of the sun porch, and do a perfect (to our minds) reenactment of the evening's matches while our two fans cheered and booed from their bed.

Eventually our house became a gathering place for many men in the business. They'd come by to pick up Donn once he was wrestling professionally, to work out on the sun porch, or just to visit with the family.

One of these was Yukon Eric. His "lats" were so huge that his arms couldn't lie flat against his sides. I remember him bare chested, pulling up in his big-finned Cadillac convertible and leaving it in the middle of the street because he'd never learned how to park.

Or Wild Bill Zimm (shortened from Zimmovich), who'd gone to art school and wrote poetry and songs. He lived with us for a while. One day I was sent to fetch something from the attic and had to pass by his third-floor room to get there. He was away on a wrestling tour, and I couldn't resist peeking in. His guitar was in the corner, and sheet music was scattered about. In another corner was a stand with a turntable, and on it an unfinished head of a young girl that he was making out of clay. It was beautiful; it made me sense his presence in the room. I left, feeling like an intruder. When I turned to look back, the head looked at me, its unfinished lips slightly parted. I'll never forget it.

Or Steve Stanlee, "Mr. America." He stayed with us a long time. Before any of us got into the business, we used to watch Steve on television.

A gentle man with the strength of a horse, Steve lifted weights religiously. Once he rang in the New Year doing bench presses with a heavily laden Olympic bar. He never missed a health-food or protein-pill fad, including something called Deterge, which was supposed to clean the bacteria from your intestines. The trouble was, according to those who tried it, the stuff took most of your intestines with it.

Steve had the biggest calf muscles I'd ever seen. He told me that when he was a kid, he was playing in a garbage dump and fell, cutting one calf badly. His pants were so soaked with blood that he was afraid to go home, and when he finally did, his mother saw a nearly severed leg. On his adult calf that cut measured only about three inches.

Steve Stanlee, "Mr. America"

In the ring Steve wore gorgeous short jackets with huge puffy sleeves. They were full of piping, sequins, spangles. It was hard to say which dazzled more: his smile, the sequins—or his long blond hair. He and his brother, Gene (also known as "Mr. America"), bleached the hell out of their hair. Steve used to take a bath in foul-smelling stuff to get *everything* blond.

In a sense, I guess, I grew up in a kind of circus. Wrestling professionally was nearly inevitable.

Sid and Dutch

We always called my father by his first name: Sid. He wanted it that way. He was never a big man. He told me that when he was in World War I on guard duty in France, General Pershing, commander of the Allied Expeditionary Force, rode by in a staff car, looked at him, and asked his aide, "Who's the Boy Scout?" Sid was full-grown then, too.

Another time in France, he rode an army mule into Paris. He was sitting on it backward, leaning over, holding its tail up to his ear like a telephone receiver and talking into its asshole. That stunt got him into an army show troop, and he spent the rest of the war entertaining French orphans, pretending to get his hand stuck in a jar.

In his heart Sid never quit show business, even though his career ended with World War I in 1918. He was always onstage. He loved parties and in the middle of them would often sneak out to the bathroom, where he'd patiently tear toilet paper into long strips, wet one end of each, and painstakingly press them onto his face: nose, chin, and—most important—his eyelids. He'd look in the mirror like an old vaudevillian and give it an audition—blinking his eyes, making the strips flutter. Then, satisfied, he'd make his grand reentrance into the thick of things, blinking like crazy.

Even before the war Sid was traveling the country, selling jewelry. He could remember the names of all the hotels he'd stayed in from Minneapolis, Minnesota, to Fargo, North Dakota. Once he was discharged from the army, he joined his father and brothers in Lewin Brothers, the first credit store in Buffalo.

Sid loved to tell how he could talk people into buying jewelry they didn't really need. A young couple would come into the store, looking for a toaster. The young woman might pause for a moment to look at the diamond rings. Sid would whisk a velvet-lined drawer of rings from under the glass counter, just to show her the diamonds up close. He'd talk points, facets, and foms. (Whatever a fom was, it wasn't in the dictionary.)

Sid would know in an instant which ring the young woman wanted, and it was out of its velvet slot and placed on her finger. You'd think Sid had just proposed! Then he'd take the couple outside so they could see the stone's color in the daylight, all the while talking in a voice like honey.

Back behind the counter, he'd do the figures for them on the monthly payments—upside down for him, right side up for them. And the couple would walk arm in arm out of the store, gazing at the twinkling treasure on her finger, owing

Above: my father, ''the Boy
Scout''; right: Sid, at right,
with the jar from his act;
below: front of Lewin Bros.

Lewin Brothers their lives for the next two years. The funny thing was, they always came back for more.

Years later Sid loved to sell to the wrestlers. They didn't know what to do with their money most of the time, and Sid was very good at relieving them of it. They loved big, flashy pinkie rings and LeCoultre diamond watches with expansion bands. And they always paid cash.

No one could figure why his three boys were so large— Sid being so small. Of course, we exercised like maniacs to get that way. The only exertion my father boasted of was bending his elbow. He used to take a terrible beating from the three of us.

Sid (who ''never washed his hair'') with brother Donn

Left: in the backyard, me throwing a dropkick; right: me practicing a flying mare on the gym mat

I remember one time we were in the backyard, working out on the mat, lifting weights, and he said something like, "I've never washed my hair—never! That's why I still have it all today." He went on and on about it. My brothers and I exchanged glances; my mother rolled her eyes heavenward. "Never washed it as a kid. Never!" Sid finished.

And that was it. Donn dropped the barbell he was doing bench presses with and got up. Mark and I circled around behind Sid. He realized he had gone too far and tried to get away. But Donn, all two hundred and thirty pounds of him, glommed poor Sid. At one hundred and thirty-five pounds, five feet, five inches, the old man didn't have a chance. Donn front-faced him and took him down onto the mat. My mother, by this time, was laughing so hard tears streamed down her cheeks. Sid was struggling, but Donn had him tied in knots.

Donn yelled, "Get the soap!" Mark and I were back in seconds with a bar of soap and the hose. We washed Sid's hair for twenty minutes—lathered it, scrubbed it. Donn held his head like a vise. There were suds everywhere. . . .

Sid had all his hair till the day he died—and still claimed he'd never washed it.

Our mother's name was Berenece. We called her Dutch. I remember her on the sun porch, my favorite place, especially in winter, when the sun would slant in its big windows all day long. She spent hours there, watching for spring in the yard, looking for fat robins; she longed to be out planting and weeding. When spring came, she'd work

Sid and Dutch in the yard

like a draft horse on the lawn, the flower beds. She'd re-arrange stones and rocks, bury tin cans around her hydran-gea bushes (for color, she said), prune the giant rosebush at the far end of the yard. She'd get so angry when all of her big sons were out there with her, too busy weight lifting to cut the grass or give her a hand.

"If you'd lift these slate stones," she said one day, "you wouldn't need to work out."

Mark and I got that duty once. We broke up slate in a vacant lot with a sledgehammer, then lugged the pieces home to make a decorative border around a flower bed. We both vowed later never to break the law. . . .

Mark could drive Dutch crazy. She got so angry with him once—I don't remember the cause, but he could always get her going—that she picked up a big roasting pan by both handles and hoisted it over her head, fully intending to brain him. He was already six feet tall, but he went into such a state of mock fear (forearm protecting his face, cringing in a corner—"Oh, God, no, Berenece . . . God, no!") that my mother doubled over with laughter and dropped the pan.

Another time Mark and I were wrestling on my bed. Dutch yelled for us to stop before we broke it—but too late. Both wooden side rails gave under the strain, and the whole thing collapsed. We heard her coming and dived under the blankets—meager protection against the eighteen-inch hard rubber truncheon that Donn, just home from the ma-rines, had bought to keep us in line. Dutch had taken it away from him but used it herself that day, just once. Boy, did it hurt!

Normally Dutch had a lot of patience with the family insanity. Especially the animals. I guess she'd had practice because even before we were born Sid used to bring home exotic pets—golden lion marmosets, cockatoos, lovebirds.

Donn was crazy about animals, too. The first pet he brought home was Cheeta, a rhesus monkey. It bit Dutch on the calf because it didn't like her red slacks. Cheeta went straight to the zoo—escaped twice—and was followed by Ellie, a capuchin monkey who rode around like a jockey on our dog's back. Count, a German shepherd, didn't seem to mind, and they both kept my mother company in the yard as she weeded, the dog lying in the shade, Ellie attached to a ring and clothesline that ran the length of the yard.

Besides me Dutch was the only one of us who could draw. She drew elephants—*only* elephants—one of the few pets we never had.

*Ellie the monkey on
the backyard clothespole*

The Sun Porch

The sun porch doubled as both gym and studio. I used to sit and draw there by the hour. Long before I started going to matches and was bitten by the wrestling bug, I wanted to be an artist. Not a policeman, fireman, or doctor—an artist. I remember working first with a metal-armed copying toy I got for Christmas, then the Magic-Pad, on which you could pull up a flap and make whatever you'd drawn disappear.

Once I'd seen a match, I began copying photographs from the wrestling programs in pencil and charcoal; next, with my first set of oil paints, illustrations out of children's books like *Two Years Before the Mast*, *My Friend Flicka*, and *Treasure Island*. Finally I got patriotic and did an oil portrait of President Harry S Truman. I copied that from the Sunday supplement, sent it to him, and received a thank-you note from the White House.

The whole family encouraged me, and I kept at it in a corner of the sun porch—all the space I needed. The rest of the sun porch was taken up with a gym mat, weights, a leather medicine ball, and a punching-bag rack hung from the wall, with speed bag attached. All this gear belonged to Donn, and once he was discharged from the marines, the porch became more or less a full-time gym. He moved in exercise benches, squat racks, and an Olympic barbell set with plates as big as locomotive wheels.

April 2, 1949

My dear Ted:

It was especially kind of you to want
the President to have the portrait, a product of
your own work. He has asked me to thank you and
to express his appreciation of your friendly
thought.

Very sincerely yours,

Rose A. Conway

ROSE A. CONWAY
Administrative Assistant
in the President's Office

Ted Lewin,
1001 Lafayette Avenue,
Buffalo 9,
New York.

Donn went into training for a bodybuilding competition and saw no reason why Mark and I shouldn't be in perfect shape, too. He had his work cut out for him: I was a butterball, and Mark was skinny. Like a good marine, Donn put us on a boot-camp regimen. We hated it. He had us running around Delaware Park on Sundays and weight lifting the rest of the week. Mark would conveniently disappear at workout time, but I'd show up conscientiously because I didn't have the guts or brains not to.

"Do ten deep knee bends with one hundred pounds," Donn would order like a drill instructor, then leave the room. I'd huff until I was red in the face, make lots of noise, but never touch the barbell.

"Did you do ten?" he'd demand when he came back.

"Uh-huh," I'd murmur, looking at the floor.

He didn't catch on, but I often wondered who I was cheating more—him or myself. After all, I was the one with the big belly.

Donn's real interest was in weight training, not wrestling. He entered the Mr. Niagara Frontier Contest and, with Mark and me cheering him on, won second place in both the bodybuilding and weight-lifting events. Not long after that, he came to the attention of Ed Don George, at that time the wrestling promoter in Buffalo.

E.D.G., as everyone called him, invited Donn to the Friday-night matches and introduced him to Steve Stanlee and Jim ("Goon") Henry. Jim told Donn in his soft Southern drawl:

Donn training just before enlisting in the marines

Left: Jim ("Goon") Henry; opposite: Donn's first publicity photo

"I want to start one guy—just one—in the business who'll amount to something before I quit." Donn was hooked.

He wrestled his first match—twenty minutes to a draw, not bad for a greenhorn—in Toronto on August 5, 1950, then moved on to Boston for three bookings and a badly broken nose.

Back in Buffalo, Donn met Danny McShain, the junior heavyweight champ. What Jim ("Goon") Henry hadn't taught him, Danny did.

Mark and I always caught Donn's matches. Once he was

on the card with Lord Blears and Captain Holmes, whose well-publicized war records included commando raids and an escape from a Japanese submarine. What a gimmick they had! Lord Blears, with his pageboy haircut and monocle, seemed to be constantly looking down his nose. Holmes,

Lord Blears, left, with Captain Holmes, riling a crowd

his manager, was impeccably upper class, with black bowler hat and walking stick.

They never failed to rile a crowd. Part of it might have been that they were British and whipped up that spirit of '76 in a lot of hearts. But most of it had to do with the mask of perfect arrogance that His Lordship would put on.

Picture this: a packed house, with just about everybody in it wanting to see Lord B. toppled and the Captain humbled, too. . . .

When the slight figure of Captain Holmes appears in the ring, the place goes wild with booing. Finally he's allowed to speak. "His Lordship requests that all men remove their hats and stand when he enters the ring." Pandemonium. The boos continue for twenty minutes until His Lordship deigns to appear. He steps regally into the ring and sets his monocle in his eye. Taking off his raiment, he signals that he's ready to proceed with the match against the Great Togo.

From the start His Lordship moves beautifully. He has a nice thing he does when he's got a headlock. He steps up on the second rope and flies off it to take his man down. But wait! After a bit he's on the bottom and in trouble. Where is Captain Holmes when he needs him? Everyone expects Holmes to pop up with instructions. But no, he's been banned from ringside for this match. His Lordship is in danger of being pinned, now. Suddenly, from the pitch-black, smoky uppermost reaches of the top balcony comes a blinking light. Two shorts, a long, two shorts, a long, and a short. What does it mean? It's a signal! His Lordship sees it. The signal comes again. Two more shorts, two longs. It's Captain Holmes with a flashlight! The crowd goes wild. His Lordship understands the coded message, recovers, is out from underneath, on top of his opponent, into his favorite hold, a cradle, and the pin. Then he's up, both hands raised in a royal victory gesture.

Captain Holmes has done it again and disappears into the nearly hysterical crowd. He's escorted quickly by special police down the labyrinth of tunnels leading to the dressing room. Meanwhile, Lord Blears has been whisked from the ring before the enraged crowd can get to him. (Escape from that Japanese sub must have been a piece of cake compared to this.)

By now all hell has broken loose. But the crowd's outrage can only be vented on an empty ring as the popcorn vendors go about their business and the next wrestlers get ready to go on. . . .

Mark and I stored that routine away. We figured it might come in handy someday.

Sandlot

When I was about fifteen and Donn was already on the road, Dutch, Sid, older sister Sallee, Mark, and I made our annual pilgrimage to Atlantic City and the New Belmont Hotel.

We were in our usual room, 401, facing the ocean. It had two twin beds, a double bed, and an army cot supplied by Charlie, the handyman. We were very comfortable and spent our days broiling on the beach, our nights looking out the window of 401 at the crowds on the boardwalk and smelling the fresh sea breezes.

We saw posters advertising the wrestling matches Friday in Convention Hall and looked for familiar names. Among them was Sammy Berg, "Mr. Canada."

On Friday morning there was a call from the lobby. It was Sammy himself. He had remembered that we were to be in Atlantic City at the time and took a chance on catching us at the hotel. He came up to 401 to fill us in on the news of his travels. But he was itching to get on the beach and show off his body, and we were itching to get seen with him—especially my sister, who loved the attention. Sammy was six feet, four inches tall and had the wide shoulders and wasp waist of a championship swimmer (his event was the butterfly), black curly hair, and a mouth full of big teeth.

I think Sammy was a little sweet on Sallee. She was a beautiful girl and tiny—five feet tall, weighing a scant one hundred pounds. The Atlantic City sun had browned her to the color of fine teak. A brown berry of a girl and a Greek god, she and Sammy made quite a twosome.

We all made our grand entrance to the beach from under the boardwalk, where the sun, shining through the boards, had turned the sand to zebra stripes. Everyone on the beach stared. My parents loved it, and Mark and I were sure everyone thought we were wrestlers, too. Sid and Dutch rented beach chairs, and we spread our blankets out in front of them. Sammy declined the blanket because no one could see him down there.

We asked him to show us some holds, since we had what looked like the beginning of a good crowd forming. He was only a kid himself, or I suppose he wouldn't have gotten drawn into it. But he agreed.

He locked horns with me first, then Mark, taking us down into the sand easily. As we got a little bolder, and more people began to wander up, we'd try taking him off his feet. He'd even let us do it once in a while. Sallee, never one to stay on the sidelines, thought it looked like fun. She stepped in, took Sammy's arm, levered it on her shoulder, and fell to her knees, turning quickly (a perfect arm drag). Sammy had no idea she knew how to do that, and his great big body flew over her into the soft sand. The crowd murmured, greatly impressed.

Sallee retired to the sidelines, triumphant. By now half the people on the beach in front of the New Belmont were watching, and we had stopped pedestrian traffic on the boardwalk.

The action got faster and more furious. Sammy was amazed at how much Mark and I knew and tried all kinds of holds, takedowns, and go-behinds—even a dropkick or two. We were all sweating profusely, and sand stuck to our bodies from head to toe. The ice-cream vendors, their heavy boxes of dry ice and Popsicles slung over their shoulders, moved in and out of the crowd, finally stopping, dropping their boxes to the beach, and sitting on them to watch. Jake, the bellboy from the New Belmont, came out and ran back to report the play-by-play to the old ladies sitting in the lobby.

We were near exhaustion and looked like three mud men from New Guinea—except it was sand, not mud, and it was in our eyes, mouths, and ears; the abrasiveness of it had caused spots of blood to ooze from elbows and knees. This exhibition was our idea, but we had no idea how to end it. Sammy did that for us. He hip-threw Mark to the sand, then me. As we got to our feet, he jumped six feet into the air and shot out two sandy feet into our two sandy heads, knocking us down like tenpins. He landed neatly on his feet, ran through the gaping crowd down to the ocean, dived into the first big breaker, and was off butterflying his way toward Europe.

Mark and I sat there with bloody elbows and ears full of sand, watching him while my parents beamed. Sallee laughed her hoarse, sexy laugh, and the crowd melted slowly away.

Dangerous Danny

The first time I saw Dangerous Danny McShain, Donn's unofficial coach in Buffalo after Jim Henry, he was leaving the ring, dripping blood from a deep gash on his forehead. The blood was pouring down his face, all over his chest, and down onto his high-topped wrestling shoes. The next time I saw him, he was parking his maroon Town and Country Chrysler convertible with wooden sides. He slammed the door and strutted—he always strutted in the ring but modified it for the street—up the stairs to our front porch. He was wearing green suede tasseled Loafers and a cream-colored Berman's of California slack suit. He loved clothes and had dozens of pairs of cow-

seventeen stitches,
head and eye

two cauliflower ears
nose broken six times
broken jaw

shoulder
dislocated twice

broken chest bone

twelve ribs broken

broken arm twice

both hands broken

torn cartilage,
both knees

broken leg

both ankles sprained

broken toe

broken ankle

Danny McShain in his prime, with a record of injuries

boy boots and slack suits of every conceivable shade. His pencil-thin mustache was surgically trimmed. Danny came for dinner—and stayed to marry my sister soon after.

Danny was a junior heavyweight, not one of the really big men. But he was shrewd and cunning and had great showmanship. When he strutted into the ring and whirled his cape with its yards of red velvet and satin, nobody cared how much he weighed.

In his early days, he had boxed and taken lots of punches. He'd bled a lot, too. The skin above his eyes was so full of scar tissue that it impaired his vision. When you'd ask him a question, he'd turn his whole head quickly, like a nervous owl, to see you. He'd been hurt by fans, too—stabbed; hit from the blind side, or "Sundayed"; struck with flying bottles and chairs; burned with cigars; stuck with hatpins.

Over his long career he broke just about every bone in his body. He had a publicity picture showing him in a wrestler's stance with labels for every injury: "two cauliflower ears," "shoulder dislocated twice," etc.

Randolph Studio, San Bernardino, California

My sister, Sallee,
a temporary blonde,
with Danny

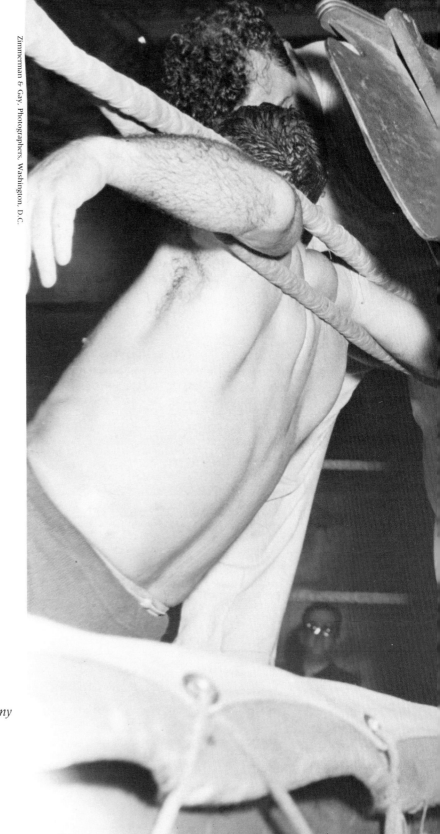

Zimmerman & Gay, Photographers, Washington, D.C.

*Dangerous Danny
at work*

One day Mark and I were working out on the gym mat in the backyard. We weren't in the business yet like Donn, but after Atlantic City we had ideas. Danny watched for a few minutes. "No, stud," he said to me, "you don't throw an elbow like that," and he stepped in to demonstrate—in his light beige Berman's. He let fly with a combination of elbow smashes that had to be felt to be believed. For a time after that I had second thoughts about wrestling professionally.

Photo Session

But second thoughts didn't last long. I needed to make some money for art school in the fall. Donn, who by that time had married and was on the road in Ohio, said he'd talk to Al Haft, the local promoter. "Okay," Haft said about me, "have the kid come on in."

At the beginning, fresh from high school, I was plenty scared. I arrived in Columbus early in June. Donn and his wife, Hattie, lived on the bottom floor of a large two-family frame house. He had arranged for me to stay next door in a rented room on the second floor of his neighbor's house. The room, at the top of the stairs, was small and pleasant. The bed had a white chenille bedspread and a mattress that was much too soft.

A professional wrestler's life had not affected Donn's fondness for collecting wild pets. Traveling with Donn and Hattie at this time was a four-month-old chimpanzee named

Donn with Sheba the lion, at the Buffalo Zoo

Jago. I guess I shouldn't have been surprised. I thought about Little Sheba, a six-week-old African lioness he'd sent home from Texas.

Sheba had arrived air freight in a special crate, and Mark and I took her to a room in the cellar where she was to stay until my parents could talk Donn out of keeping her. Before long, she was eating four pounds of horse meat a day and growing as big as a German shepherd.

One day Sheba bit me as I turned away from feeding her.

Above: Sheba and me in
the cellar; right: Donn as
Tarzan of the Apes

Donn came home from the road a few days later and said
it wouldn't have happened if I had put her food down
properly. So Mark and I watched while he showed us how.
As he turned to leave her, Sheba bounded from her corner,
grabbed him around the waist, and bit him on the butt. The
next day he called the Buffalo Zoo and asked if it would be
interested in adding a six-month-old lioness to its collection.
To everyone's relief, the zoo said yes.

So now there was Jago. He was still small and depen-
dent—and not toilet trained. They kept diapers on him all
the time. He spent most of his day sitting on Hattie's hip
with his arms around her neck, staring in her ear. Donn

was a big Edgar Rice Burroughs fan, and having Jago around made him feel like Tarzan of the Apes.

The first time I sat down to dinner with the three of them, Jago eyed me suspiciously from his perch on Hattie's hip. When I tried to make friends, he bit me and screamed. I figured he needed time to get used to me.

The next morning Donn and I drove downtown to Al Haft's wrestling office so Haft could get a look at the baby brother. Behind the office was an enormous building with two wrestling rings and one wall that was practically all glass.

Haft was a huge man. He shook my hand and looked me over front and back. I was convinced he was going to check my teeth. "Get into your trunks and shoes," he said, "and we'll take some publicity pictures."

I went into a dressing room, changed, and came out into the small room where the pictures were to be taken. I was the only one in wrestling gear. Everyone else was fully clothed. I felt naked.

The room was loaded with rough-looking characters. Some I'd seen in the ring when I was a kid. Speedy LaRance was over in one corner. He was built like an ape, with a shiny bald head. He was talking to Lenny Montana, who was as big as his name. Billy Wolfe, who managed Fabulous Moolah (one of the few women then in the business), was bending Al Haft's ear. Billy wore a snap-brimmed hat and a dapper suit with a diamond stickpin in his tie. The diamonds on his fingers glinted as he gestured with his hands.

Buddy ("Nature Boy") Rogers swaggered in wearing the suit that was his trademark—wide shoulders and vented at the sides for freer movement. He had long, bleached blond hair, he smoked big cigars, and when he talked out of the corner of his mouth, people listened. He and my brother had been selling out all over the territory. He spotted me standing there nearly naked and alone and came up to look me over. Then he called to Donn, and they began discussing my possibilities.

Finally the photographer came in. "Okay, get into a stance," he said. I did.

Buddy Rogers (who introduced me to cigars later on) said, "No, kid. Your left foot forward, not your right."

Speedy LaRance said, "Bend over a little more. You're standing up too straight."

Brother Donn said, "No, it's your right foot forward."

Lenny Montana said, "Look mean."

Al Haft said, "No, no, don't look mean. Look nice."

The bulb flashed, and the shutter snapped. We had it—a picture of a left-footed, crouching, standing, mean, nice baby wrestler.

Now we all headed for a big sunlit room with two rings. It was the first time I had actually stepped between the ropes and stood in a real ring—a long way from the old gym mat in the backyard.

I was about as sure of myself as Donn had been when Jim Goon threw him around those afternoons in Memorial Auditorium. Donn told me he had felt like a rag doll, being tossed around the ring; whenever his body hit the canvas, the thud echoed in the recesses of the hall. The poor local guy Haft had found for me was no Goon. His biggest worry was not to let my clumsiness rub off on him, as sometimes

My overcoached publicity photo

happens. I made some of the moves that I'd practiced with Mark: dropkicks, various takedowns and holds, all painstakingly gleaned from those Friday-night matches back in Buffalo.

I guess it went all right because Al Haft watched closely and finally nodded his approval. He told Donn he'd use me as much as he could. Then I showered, and we headed home for an early dinner. Donn was wrestling nearby that night.

I didn't know it, but I had one more ordeal ahead of me. Hattie greeted us at the door with Jago growing out of her hip as usual.

"How'd it go?" she asked. I smiled meekly, shrugged my shoulders, and looked at Donn. He grunted. Donn grunted a lot. I think he learned it in the marines.

We had steak and a big salad for dinner. Donn wanted to do some shopping with Hattie before the matches that night and said Jago would only complicate matters if they took him. Donn asked if I'd keep an eye out. He didn't tell me it was the first time they'd ever left Jago behind.

Hattie removed him from her hip—not without difficulty—and handed him to me. Then they left for the store in Donn's new Hudson Hornet, and it was just me and Jago there in the living room. He was sitting on my hip, wearing diapers, with his long hairy arms clinging to my neck.

Since his usual hip had just gone out the door, he turned to see whose he was sitting on. He looked up at my face with his shiny black eyes. His ears were huge and pink and stuck out like open car doors. He knitted his beetle brow, and the highlights in his eyes disappeared. It was dawning on him that he'd been deserted. Then he opened his mouth as wide as he could and began to scream piteously, all the while tugging at his awesome bottom teeth with one hairy hand. He screamed and screamed. It was ear shattering.

I had no idea what to do; I'd never chimp-sat before. I walked around the dining-room table with him screaming and tugging at those bottom teeth as if he was trying to yank them out.

I talked soothingly to him. He screamed louder. Finally I set him down on his feet, holding on to one of his hands. He pulled me over to the window and looked at the spot where the Hudson had been. He screamed even louder. I started to walk around the table again, holding his damp hairy hand in mine. It was a toss-up as to which of us was the more miserable.

Maybe he'd like to be in the yard, I thought. Hand in hand, we headed for the back door. We walked a big circle

Jago and me,
momentary friends

around the yard, him with his funny rolling gait, dragging his free hand's knuckles on the ground when he wasn't pulling at his teeth—while screaming nonstop.

I could see neighbors looking out of their windows and over their back fences. Jago now decided he'd rather bite my hand than hold it. I knew I couldn't let go or Tarzan's eight-hundred-dollar fantasy would disappear over the fences and into the trees. But I couldn't stand the pain either, so I dragged him back to the screen door, opened it, and set him inside, still screaming for all he was worth. I slammed the door and leaned against it, half-deaf but relieved.

Suddenly the screaming stopped. It was so quiet so fast that the silence was deafening. For several minutes I heard not a sound. I began to get uneasy. I opened the screen door and peered into the dark hallway. No Jago. Once my eyes adjusted from the sun, I walked down the hall, past the kitchen, and into the living room.

There he was, sitting naked on the back of the couch, gazing out of the window. I looked on the floor. His diaper was there with a huge smelly load in it. Leading from the diaper were brown chimp footprints that went across the floor and as far up the wall as he'd been able to run before the color gave out. Fainter footprints marked the route back to the diaper for a fresh supply. A little stamping in the mess, and off again with nice fresh prints, out and up the wall in all directions.

Just then Jago spotted the Hudson easing into a parking spot. He jumped off the couch and was waiting at the door as the familiar hip of my sister-in-law came back into his life.

So began my career as a professional wrestler.

PART TWO

Donn and me: tag partners

Learning the Ropes

Al Haft was true to his promise and booked me three or four nights a week. At first these were for tag-team matches mainly, with Donn as my partner, wrestling another pair of guys. We took turns, so there were not more than two opponents in the ring at a time. I could tag out if I got into trouble, was at a loss for a next move, or was just plain tired. All I had to do was get to Donn, who'd be off to the side, and tag his hand; he would replace me in the ring.

It didn't take long to learn the ropes—literally. At first they seemed in the way, confining. Then I realized the ropes gave a third dimension to the ring. They enabled you to bounce and fly up as well as across. They could be used like a catapult or a stepladder.

In tag-team matches, the ropes added the dimension of excitement, too, by keeping you from your partner. I learned how to stir up the crowd by grabbing the end of the two-foot length of rope tied to the ring's corner post—its length determined how far you could legally stray from the corner. Then, pulling it as taut as I could, I would lean way over the top rope of the ring. Donn, held by his opponent, would reach from the center of the ring for a tag. The more I leaned out to tag him, the more the crowd liked it; I'd lean until my feet left the ground and my body was balanced on the top rope. Donn would make a lunge, and our fingertips, only an inch away now, would finally touch. The fans loved it, so I did the stunt more and more often. I was learning to get the feel of an audience and to control their reactions.

One night in Mansfield, Ohio, my opponent on the other side of the ring decided to steal my gimmick. His partner reached for a tag. He stretched as far out as he could over the ropes, aping me, until his feet left the ground and he was balanced perfectly on the top rope. I latched onto the top rope on my side and began to shake it violently. The shock waves traveled around until they reached him. He flailed with his hands and feet to keep his balance; I shook harder; he flailed harder, like a drowning man. Then he fell forward in a somersault into the ring.

In seconds he was up and storming around. The referee tried to push him out, but he argued and headed for Donn. Donn gave me the signal, and I was in. So was our opponent's partner. We were all in there, throwing punches, tackles, dropkicks. The referee ran for a corner to get out of the traffic.

"Headlock," Donn yelled to me. Somehow I figured out what to do. We ran at each other, pulling our opponents with us. We bumped their heads, and they both fell neatly backward, the soles of their feet facing each other. The crowd went wild.

Donn looked at me and said over the din, "Do you know the rowboat?" I shook my head no. "Do what I do," he said. He sat on the mat and grabbed one ankle of each man.

I have Bull Curry in a headlock.

I did the same on the opposite side. We were now facing each other with our feet bottoms touching. "Row!" Donn told me, so we leaned back, using their legs for oars, and rowed. Did those guys yell and squirm! We sat back up, relieving the pressure on their groins. "Row!" Donn repeated. I rowed for all I was worth. Now the crowd was chanting, "Row! Row!" We fell in with the rhythm of it.

Donn said, "Okay, let go and do a back roll . . . now!" We let go together, rolling neatly backward up onto our feet. "Get out!" he said. I scampered out of the ring and grabbed my two-foot length of rope. Donn made a diving leap onto one of our opponents and pinned him. The ref was there in a flash and counted to three. The match was over.

The Lewin brothers hugged each other. Donn picked up baby brother by the waist for the crowd's approval. They loved it. Our opponents were up now, stomping about, hitting the ropes with both hands, threatening the referee, yelling insults at us and the crowd.

"Stick with me," Donn said. And just then our opponents charged us. We met them with elbow smashes—and they faltered. "Headlock," Donn yelled, and again we ran them across the ring and butted their heads together. Down they went. "C'mon," Donn cried, and jumped over them and ran to our corner. He grabbed the top rope, leaped neatly over it, and landed on the apron. I followed, catching my feet in the top rope and almost breaking my neck. But he caught me.

We headed down the ringside stairs and ran past the happy throng of faces. In the dressing room everyone crowded around Donn, telling him how good "the kid" looked.

Donn and me, with someone's bowling trophy brought in for the photo

"Of course," he said, mussing my hair. "He's my baby brother."

As we started to strip for the showers, he stuck a huge lump of Red Man tobacco into his cheek, then offered some to me. Hell, I thought, why not? The tobacco juice went through me like greased lightning. I didn't even make it to the shower—and swore off the stuff for all time after that.

But chewing agreed with Donn. We headed out in the Hudson that night, giving Speedy LaRance and Danny

*Donn with me
before a match*

O'Shocker a ride. Brother Donn, his cheek full of Red Man, would reach over occasionally to the mason jar he kept on the front seat, unscrew the top, and spit into it. It was lethal-looking stuff.

We stopped to eat at a favorite place and had big salads and sausage sandwiches and beer in frozen mugs. I was finding out there was always a "favorite place" where the owner liked wrestlers, felt we were good for business. In every town they'd load on the food, sometimes give us free drinks, and never "crack wise."

Here we are, I thought that night, like family—not just Donn and me, but all the other guys, too. In the ring we'd throw one another all over the place, yell insults, punch and kick, sometimes hurt each other. Then we'd pile into cars together. If this is how it's going to be, I thought, I like it fine.

We dropped the others off at their hotel and headed home. Donn always liked to get home. He'd drive half the night rather than stay in a hotel. He parked the Hudson and walked up onto his front porch, bag in hand. He took the chew out of his mouth and threw it like mulch into the bushes. "See you in the morning, Teddle. We'll find out where we're booked the rest of the week."

I went quietly up the stairs to my room in the darkened house next door. I opened my bag and took my damp wrestling shoes out to dry. Then I slipped under the sheets without removing the chenille bedspread and fell asleep, smiling.

Greenhorn

Funny, I never really felt like a beginner. If I stopped to think about it—being thrown around a ring in front of thousands of people, doing flying tackles and dropkicks—it didn't seem possible. I was way too shy. In high school I couldn't finish a one-paragraph speech for an assembly honoring my retiring art teacher—got the first two words out, saw all those faces looking at me, and turned into Tom Tomato. The teacher herself rescued me, eighty-year-old Mrs. Wieffenbach. She came to the mike, put her arm around my waist, and said to the audience, "He draws better than he talks."

But wrestling audiences never frightened me. And every day on the tour that summer I was picking up tricks.

One night I saw Speedy LaRance put a large pad of rubber in the back of his trunks. I asked him why. "Got a bad back," he said, "and this helps. It's what cleaning women kneel on, and it's got just the right amount of give."

I told him my heel was sore; I'd bruised it going over in a flying mare. That's the hold in which your opponent takes your head and flips you over his shoulders. He said all the boys used rubber pads like his in their shoes, cut to the shape of the heel. "You'll never bruise it again," he promised. (He also told me to turn my body slightly when going over in a mare or hip throw and to land on the side of my thigh and foot—never on the point of the heel.)

I learned to exaggerate moves: to fall to the mat, hitting it hard with my arms to make a "splash," and to yell, which releases the air out of you and loosens the body to absorb shocks better.

And I learned more about the rings. The good ones have great spring near the corners but not in the center, where the supports are. Bad rings are too rigid. If you slam someone to the mat in the right place in a good ring, he'll bounce six or eight inches, and a bounce makes the slam much more exciting to watch. When I was on the receiving end, I learned to lift myself and arch my back—the best way not to get hurt.

Flying *out* of the ring is the most dangerous thing. You never know where you're going to land—or on what. I learned how to land after throwing a dropkick so I didn't hurt myself worse than my opponent. And I learned that if my fingers were about to be stomped on, I should flatten them out fast (either that or forget about art school in the fall).

With each match I was feeling more confident. But even with all the tricks that Speedy LaRance and others taught me, my body still took a beating. I had bruises everywhere,

I'm about to give Bull Curry a knee lift.

and brush burns on my elbows and knees so bad that sometimes it was impossible to sleep.

I started having single matches and traveling with other
guys in Ohio, then Kentucky, West Virginia, even Indiana,
while Donn was booked elsewhere. He stayed on in Ohio
and had matches with Buddy ("Nature Boy") Rogers that
became legendary.

In one of these the ring was set up on the stage of an old
theater, and the distance from the top rope to the floor of
the orchestra pit must have been fifteen feet. Donn was
coming off the ropes with a tackle when Buddy bent from

the waist and caught Donn on his back. Buddy stood up quickly and back-dropped Donn over the top rope to the floor fifteen feet below. Twelve years and much agony later, Donn had to have the two disks he damaged that night fused into one in a three-hour operation.

In the old days cauliflower ears were a wrestler's badge of courage. I'd heard that greenhorns, in order to look tough, used to bang their ears on a radiator to get them started. They couldn't wait for the injury to happen in the natural course of events. Maybe so . . . Almost everyone got cauli-flower ears anyway. A punch, a dropkick, an elbow, anything could start an ear swelling with blood. Then it'd be sore as a boil. Donn used to carry a hypodermic syringe in his bag (he practiced medicine without a license for years); he'd do ear surgery on anyone—even himself. He'd wash the ear with alcohol and then stick the needle in and draw off syringe after syringe of blood until it went flat. Of course, one punch and it'd be swollen right up again.

I got a carbuncle behind my ear once, I suppose from one of the filthy mats in the outdoor shows. The boys all looked at me like I was a leper. They tried to wrestle me without touching me. So Dr. Donn came to the rescue. He took a double-edge Gillette blade, dipped it in alcohol, and slit the awful thing open. Then he took a Coke bottle he'd been heating and put the neck over the open sore to draw out the

Opposite: a wrestling program, with Donn's name misspelled, as it often was; below: I have the Bull by the ears.

pus. When I screamed in pain, he told me to shut up, said he'd seen guys hurt a lot worse in the marines who'd sat and smoked a cigarette.

"I'm not a marine," I said. "And I don't smoke."

Donn stayed on the road for twenty years before finally quitting the business to stay home with Hattie and his ocelot, boa constrictor, and an iguana named Iggy. Iggy used to climb into the Christmas tree, turn green, and stay there without moving until New Year's.

A Double Life

In the fall of 1952, I began formal art training at Pratt Institute in Brooklyn, New York. I'd made some money over the summer, but Brooklyn was a lot more expensive than Buffalo. I needed some night work to make ends meet.

Every day I had classes in two-dimensional design, three-dimensional design, and figure drawing. Around me, the light-filled, high-ceilinged studio would be electric with concentrated effort—students in paint-spattered jeans looking at the nude model, studying her, then plunging brushes into gobs of oil paint and applying it to canvas. I would see a great play of light and shadow—in a sense, not so different from what I'd seen in the charged, dramatic atmosphere of a wrestling arena. The medium was different, that's all. Wrestling and painting—a double life, but with no great disparity between the halves. I felt as fulfilled and complete after a good match as I did after making a successful picture.

Center of the Wrestling Universe

When I left Ohio, I had with me a letter of introduction from Al Haft in Columbus to Toots Mondt, the promoter in New York. I took the letter to the address I'd been given: the Holland Hotel on Forty-second Street near the Port Authority bus terminal.

Everything, I discovered, revolved around one second-floor office there. A single phone call or visit, and your life was planned for you for the next week. The "book," in which men's names were moved about like the pieces on a chessboard, held the grand plan. Each of the dates marked represented a town, a big one or a little one, it didn't matter—they were all equally important. Five matches, ten men. If Antonio Rocca was working in Madison Square Garden on Monday before a crowd of twenty-five thousand, he was in Sparta, New Jersey, with a crowd of two thousand five hundred on Tuesday. Matches were all the same in the book.

My first year of art school I saw a lot of the Holland Hotel.

The lobby was early-forties bad taste with a worn-out Oriental carpet and even more worn-out plastic chairs and couches pushed back against the walls. The bellboys were worn-out, too, and suitably cynical, but the wrestlers were special to them.

I could always tell if one of the guys was coming down the street by watching pedestrians beyond the thick plate-glass windows of the coffee shop where all the wrestlers waited for their rides. Amazed, they'd stop dead in their tracks and gape. Perhaps it was Haystack Calhoun, all six hundred pounds of him in his overalls, with a heavy chain—horseshoe attached—slung around his neck. He was only in his twenties then, but as big as a Belgian horse.

Left: Toots Mondt;
opposite: Haystack Calhoun at 650 pounds

He'd stop to sign autographs for the fans on the sidewalk, then one ancient bellboy would open the glass door for him and grab his big heavy wrestling bag.

"Hi, Stacks. Where're you working tonight?"

Haystack would smile his sweet smile, put his arm around the bellboy, and hug him, smothering him in all that flesh and denim. . . .

Or perhaps it was Waldeck ("Killer") Kowalski. I remember a cab pulling up across the street from the hotel and a lean six-foot, seven-inch body unfolding itself from the backseat. The man saw us through the window and waved—glad to see everyone. We watched the passersby stare up at him and nudge one another forward to ask him for an autograph.

"We saw you in our hometown once. We're from Lexington, Kentucky." He'd sign and head on into the lobby.

"Hi, Killer. Where're you working?"

"Hi, Killer."

"Hi, Killer."

Bellboy, desk clerk, switchboard operator.

He'd come into the coffee shop.

"Hi, Wally." Waldeck Kowalski, the meanest, kindest human being you'd ever want to meet. He was as gaunt and lean as a Southern preacher, and a strict vegetarian. It was a wonder how he maintained his weight of two hundred and eighty pounds on lettuce and carrots. . . .

Or perhaps we'd be drinking coffee and the elevator doors would open across the lobby. We'd hear an unmistakable

Killer Kowalski, Bridgeport, Connecticut

guttural Russian accent and in would come Kola Kwariani, "the Russian Bear." He'd pause in the doorway for maximum effect, look over his rimless glasses with crinkled eyes, spread his huge hairy arms out as if to embrace the whole roomful at once, and say, "Hello, boys!" Then he'd flash a big smile that gleamed like his granite head.

"Is everyone here? We can get going."

The bellboys would join us on the sidewalk, admiring us all like proud parents. Again passersby would stare. Then the guys who were driving would go for their cars in the parking lot across the street.

I always jumped in with Kola.

Kola

When I first showed up at the Holland, it was Kola I talked to. He was the keeper of the "book."

His English was delivered in a near whisper and was almost unintelligible. I was the only one who could make it out most of the time. I told him I was in art school and hoped to be booked a few nights a week to pay expenses. Art school—that's all he had to hear. It turned out he had a fine artistic temperament. He was, physically, a painter's dream, with a massive bald head and a neck like a bull's. The hair so lacking up top was abundant everywhere else. It curled over his oaklike forearms, pushed out of his open shirtfront. On one side of his head there was a deep depression about eight inches long—the work of a cossack's saber from the old days in Russian Georgia.

We talked and talked about art and politics and Russia and wrestling and women and tuberculosis. He had had six wives. All had died of TB—he said he was a carrier.

And we talked about eating. Especially eating. He ate so much once that he had to sit in a tubful of cold water to keep from passing out. One time he said to me, "You ever eat Greek food?" I hadn't, so he took me around the corner from the Holland, downstairs to a Greek cafeteria.

He ordered retsina, the resinated Greek wine, and said softly, "Drink!" The stuff tasted like turpentine. He ordered lamb's head. "You have to eat the eyes," he told me. "Best part." I ate the eyes.

Kola told me one day that he was going to Hollywood. I thought he was kidding, but he wasn't. Going to be in a movie, he said, directed by a friend of his, Stanley Kubrick, a young man nobody had heard of at the time. Kola was really excited about it. Six days later he was home in New York, and we were in the backseat of a car headed for matches in Hartford. He told me his part had been written into the movie for him—the character loved to play chess and was an old-time pro wrestler with the strength of an elephant. That was Kola. His movie, *The Killing*, turned out to be a minor classic.

Kola lived on the twelfth floor of the Holland. I'd done a drawing of him, and I wanted him to have it. I got off the elevator on twelve and made my way through the dreary corridor to his door. His wife answered it (perhaps she was his seventh? I didn't ask). He barked at her in Russian, and

Kola in two stills from The Killing; *left: a close-up with Sterling Hayden*

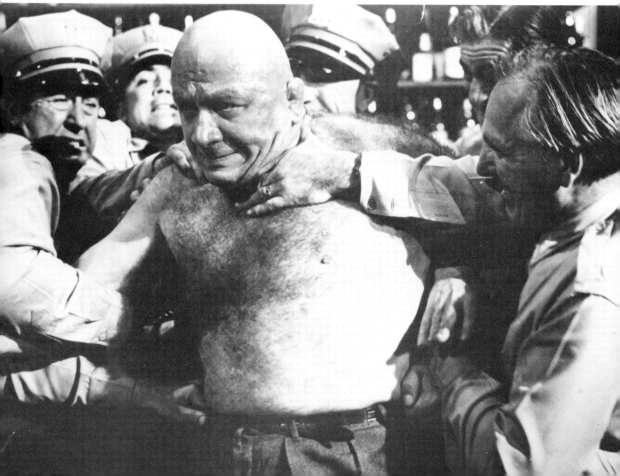

she withdrew to a tiny kitchen. The apartment was dark, and I peered into the small main room through a beaded curtain. He sat on the bed in his undershorts like a Russsian Buddha, great granite head glistening.

"Come in, come in," he said softly. The walls were full of paintings and drawings in gold frames with lights over them—the main source of illumination in the room. The ceiling seemed to be hung with drapes, like the tent of a Tatar. A brass samovar for making tea gleamed in the corner.

I showed Kola the drawing. He looked over his glasses, lifted a huge hand, and pointed a finger at me, saying, "You know, Ted, you have the touch, the gift. You will be great."

I believed him absolutely. I was seventeen years old.

Laurel Garden

In 1952, Kola Kwariani had his last professional match with me at Laurel Garden in Newark, New Jersey.

From the beginning Laurel Garden was one of my favorite shots. Maybe it was because I was a new kid, and it seemed colorful. It never paid much money, but there was something about the place.

I'd take the subway from school in Brooklyn to the Port Authority in Manhattan; from there it was half an hour by bus to Newark. The same fans were on hand every week. I always felt at home when I walked through the long, open front lobby with the box office off to the side. Inside the hall

Kola with fans in the bleachers, watching the matches at Laurel Garden

there was a balcony that ran across the back and down both sides to a stage. The place smelled musty—like the inside of an old trunk. The ring was in the center, on a very old wooden floor, and was surrounded by fifteen or twenty rows of wooden chairs. Bleachers were set up on the stage, alongside some ancient props and scenery. Matches were televised from Laurel Garden every Friday night.

Jack Pfeffer was the promoter, and he always oversaw everything in the tiny, filthy dressing room. He was an incredible character. Small and slight, about sixty years old, he looked like a mad violinist. He had long yellow-gray hair and a big hooked nose. He had very long dirty fingernails, especially on his left little finger. He'd insert this nail into a nostril of that big hooked nose and casually remove whatever was troubling him. Then he'd drag the finger through his hair to clean it off, all the while talking, calling you—and everybody—"baby doll."

The dressing room was jammed so tightly with huge men and officials that you could barely move. I was unlucky enough once to be standing behind the door when one of Jack's "discoveries" for that week, Franky Dallo (all four hundred pounds of him), came barging through it. I was swept aside and pinned against a red-hot radiator. I had trunks on, and my legs were bare. The encounter branded me with three vertical burns down my thigh that stayed for weeks.

There was an old black ring doctor—can't remember his name. A fine gentleman. And also a small fat man with huge thyroid eyes; he gave cardiograms, which were required for a license to wrestle in New Jersey.

I used to love to take friends from art school to Laurel Garden—always made me chuckle to have them see me in that strange setting. One friend had an art store near Pratt. He figured he knew a little bit about painting and art because, after all, he sold the supplies. After my match I went out to ringside and sat with him. The place had worked its spell. He looked around in awe, turned to me, and said, "How would you do it, kid, in browns and greens?"

"In this corner!"
—Laurel Garden

The Summer of '53

During the summer of 1953, I went back upstate to work with Ed Don George out of Buffalo. E.D.G. was happy to help a kid pay his way through college.

He worked "spot shows" in the damnedest places: ballparks, fairgrounds, stock-car tracks, high school gyms—anywhere he could pull in a few people. The most curious was in a cow pasture.

We got there in the late afternoon. The matches were going on early because there were no lights. In fact, there were no seats—only a ring set up out in the middle of this field—no dressing rooms, no nothing. We changed in the backseats of the cars. And the really odd thing was that people paid to walk through an imaginary gate for the privilege of sitting on the grass among the cow flops to watch us. If you didn't pay, you could watch from outside the imaginary gate a foot or two farther back. Everyone paid—all the local people, farmers and the like.

Sometimes we'd land in a baseball stadium from the old International League. These ballparks were made of concrete and looked like ancient Roman ruins, full of cracks and holes. Water was always dripping into the dressing rooms from somewhere. When we arrived, we'd all rifle through the beat-up lockers, looking for treasures. And once in a while we'd strike it rich. Somebody would have left part of a uniform or a baseball glove—and always there were stashes of blue ointment.

Occasionally the office would run an indoor show in a nice new auditorium—in Syracuse, for instance. It almost felt like being in a hospital ward in the dressing rooms there, they were so clean. Somehow those matches never had the raw feeling of the ones out in the boondocks, where the crowd was less inhibited, better to work. The people in those little towns really let loose. Their necks would get so red that they'd glow. Audiences in the country—even more than the city fans—were the fourth member of the troupe: the two wrestlers, the referee, and them.

I remember getting my gear on one night and waiting alone in the dressing room for my match. It was one of those dripping dressing rooms under the bleachers in a ballpark, with hundreds of fans sitting above me. I could feel the pulse of the match through the pounding of their feet. I could tell what had just happened in the ring by the decibel level of their screams.

I walked out into the night with a towel thrown over my bare shoulders and looked up at the black, star-spangled sky. I walked to the edge of the grandstand, where I could just see the glow of the floods shining down on the ring. It was snowing bugs. I listened. The crowd fell silent and sullen with only an occasional grumble. I could picture the ring action: the favorite was having the stuffing kicked out of him. All of a sudden the excitement of the crowd grew. It grew, and the fans started screaming encouragement to their hero. I knew in the ring he was reviving, pulling himself up from defeat. The marks were lifting him, plugging him into their energy. The roar was tremendous. Without seeing it,

I knew he was up. He was coming back. He was whaling that villain, giving it back to him in spades. I smiled and felt a tingle of excitement crawl over my flesh. My turn was coming, my union with those hundreds out there. I was hooked.

I went back to the empty dressing room to warm up. The whole stadium was shaking with the stamping and screaming of the crowd. Then the bell. It was over. Silence. The announcement of the winner. Great applause and general jubilation. Their hero had come out on top.

The wrestlers came back into the dressing rooms one at a time, sweating and dirty. The villain, covered with beer and popcorn from the gauntlet he'd just run, was in my dressing room. He sat down, caught his breath, and looked over at me.

"How was it?" he asked.

"Great," I said. "Great."

Jimmie Mitchell, "the Black Panther," and I had a match one night on the fairgrounds of a little upstate town. It was really cold for early summer, and it was pouring rain. The ringside had been reduced to mush. Everyone who held tickets went and sat in the covered grandstand, where the day before they'd watched horse-pulling contests. I don't ever remember being so cold. Poor Jimmie was shivering so badly his teeth were banging together. His black skin was gooseflesh, and his bald head had rivulets of rain streaming from it. The canvas that covered the ring mat was soggy and full of puddles—very dangerous.

The ring was illuminated by six sets of floodlights on top of very tall poles. The people in the bleachers sat stoically, just sat there and watched two grown men—one black, one white—shiver, slip, slide, and fall with great splashes into the puddles in the ring. They watched them fall off the apron and into the mud below, then climb back into the ring, both of them black now, until the driving rain, washing away the mud, miraculously changed one back to white.

Finally, mercifully, the referee cut the match at sixteen minutes instead of twenty, so we could get out of there. Nobody noticed anyway.

It was no decision, a draw. Jimmie, shaking like a leaf now, jumped down from the apron into ankle-deep glue and slogged his way to the dressing room under the grandstand. I followed right behind, head down against the buffeting rain, watching my feet in high-topped wrestling shoes sinking out of sight in the mud.

In the dressing room, Jimmie said, "Did you see those idiots sitting out there in the pouring rain?" *Those* idiots? I thought to myself. I shrugged my shoulders and jumped, shoes and all, into the cold shower to wash off the mud— and the manure from yesterday's horse pull.

Skippy Jackson

In June of 1953 poor Mark had yet to leave Buffalo for the first time. Being home alone was misery for him. He badgered Dutch and Sid constantly.

One day Dangerous Danny called from California. "Send him out," he said. "I'll get him booked for the summer."

Mark went, promising to come back to school in the fall.

A box of cigars to the right person got him a license because, legally, he was too young—a baby-faced high school boy with lots of black hair. He called himself Skippy Jackson.

Dutch always felt a little guilty about letting him go. Like Donn when he joined the marines, Mark was only sixteen. Except for quick visits, he never really went home again; his vagabond life took him far away.

3:00 A.M., one day in 1962:

Riinnng! I fumble in the dark.

"Uhh . . . hello?"

"This is the overseas operator. Will you accept a collect call?"

"From who?"

"Mark Lewin."

"Jesus! Okay."

"Hi!"

"Are you all right?"

"Yeah. What's going on?"

"It's three in the morning here."

"Business is great. Selling out every night. How about you? How's the art business?"

"Fine. Where are you calling from?"

"Sydney, Australia."

"Collect? Jesus!"

3:45 A.M., spring 1963:

Riinnng! Riinnng!

"Hello?" (in a rough, middle-of-the-night voice)

Donn and Mark in the early sixties

"Hi. What's happening?"

"Hi. It's almost four in the morning here."

"Things are going fine for me. I'm training like crazy, got nineteen-inch arms and a new gimmick—Maniac Mark."

"Wonderful. Where are you calling from?"

"The Peninsula Hotel."

"In Hong Kong?"

"Yeah."

"Thank God it's not collect!"

4:30 A.M., later in 1963:

Riinnng! Riinnng!

Left: Mark as Skippy Jackson; below: Mark, years later, with a great fan, ''Miss Lillian'' Carter— they're demonstrating his secret weapon, the ''third eye'' (Mark's version is correct).

"Hello?"

"Hold on, please. This is the overseas operator."

"Hi."

"Hi, how are you? Gimme a minute to wake up."

"I'm fine. Business is great. Ever since we got here reporters have been following us around, taking pictures—front-page stuff. I'll send you a paper, but you won't be able to read it."

"How come?"

"It's in Japanese."

"Where the hell are you calling from?"

"Tokyo. Don't worry. I'm paying for it. King Curtis is with me and sends his regards—so does Baba the Giant."

"Don't forget to send the newspaper."

5:15 A.M., early 1965:

Riinnng! Riinnng!

"Hello?" (big yawn)

"Hi."

"You sound like you're around the corner. Where are you?"

"Auckland—biz is great. Got some great training partners here and have been doing two workouts a day."

"Auckland? New Zealand?"

"Yeah, beautiful place. You'd love it. The whole country looks like a national park."

"How long will you be there?"

"A few weeks. Then on to Fiji and Korea for a few shots. I'll be in Tokyo at Christmastime."

"Sounds great. Call me at Christmas . . . collect."

Bozo Brown

I spent a lot of the summer of '53 traveling with Frank Hickey, alias Bozo Brown. Everyone loved Frank (they called him Mother Hickey), but no one wanted to travel with him. He used to take all the back roads and stay at out-of-the-way cabins far from any "hang arounds," as he called curious fans. The other boys would stay in town, have a good time, sleep late, catch a movie, enjoy a big salad at two or three in the afternoon, and head for the next town. That's what I wanted to do, too, of course. But I was with Frank.

His routine never varied. We'd leave the matches and drive in his big old Cadillac late into the night, until we'd find some God-forsaken motel, get the owner up from a sound sleep, and sign in.

Once I had to share a bed with Frank because there was only one vacant cabin. He was a big man, two hundred and seventy pounds, and didn't leave much room for me. He told me before we went to sleep to cover up and be careful of "drafts on the chest. They're what killed former champ Everett Marshall," he said.

We'd always get up at the crack of dawn (while the rest of the boys in town were still asleep) and head to the woods for a hike. Frank always carried a big stick. "In case of dogs," he told me. When we got back, the motel owner would be up and around. Over the years some motel owners had

Opposite: Bozo Brown in his gold cape (see also the back of the jacket)

gotten to know Frank; they knew better than to try talking to him about the business—about whether wrestling was all fake or what—or about anything personal. To the inquisitive Frank always said in his high squeaky voice, "No questions!" And then we'd spend the day helping out around the place. Frank loved to paint, do repairs, cut grass. Keep things "neat, neat, guy," he'd say to me, while I'd be wondering what the boys were doing back in civilization.

Frank loved cars. He hoped to open a little garage in California one day and build racing cars. He had a publicity picture taken of himself wearing his long wool tights and top and mask, sitting behind the wheel of a racing car he built.

Opposite page: Frank in cape and matching hood; above: two views of him in his racing car; right: Frank in his shop

He also loved the circus with a passion and never missed a local show. He knew the performers by name and showed me once how one man did a dozen different acts in an afternoon, changing from his acrobat costume to work the dancing bears. Most of all Frank liked to "check the rigging" of the high-wire act.

I remember stopping with him to get a salad at a roadside diner on the way to a match. The waitress eyed him curiously and then retreated to the kitchen to talk to the cook. Then he peered out at Frank's cauliflower ears and great bulk; the two of them whispered back and forth till finally she returned to our table.

"Say, don't I know you? I've seen you on TV. You're a rassler, right?"

"Nope!" he answered (he never let on). "Just a big fat truck driver." Then, trying to convince her, he added, barely loud enough to hear, "Damn rig was kickin' sand on me in fifth gear, but I got 'er out of the ditch anyway." And he winked at me.

We'd get to the matches very early so Frank could check out the place—usually a filthy dressing room in one of those small-town ballparks, or maybe the basement of an American Legion hall. He'd check the hot water, the condition of the ring (hard or soft), the turnbuckles on the ropes—like a circus flier testing his rigging. That done, he'd spend thirty minutes neatly laying out newspapers all around where he was to sit and change. And finally he'd produce his costume for the evening—starting with very high-topped wrestling shoes, custom-made to his design in New York City. They were color coordinated with the rest of his outfit. "Goddamn beautiful!" he'd say.

Next would come long wool tights with leather knee pads and a full top with sleeves and matching hood—wool with leather trim. He had a trunk full of those hoods; they covered his face and head, with cutouts for eyes, nose, and mouth, and they laced up the back. Last but not least came the full-length satin cape, which he tied at his neck with a length of heavy gold braided drapery cord. The whole thing *was* "goddamn beautiful!" It took him a full hour to put it all on, and then he'd sit there on his newspaper throne and hold court as the rest of the boys would dribble in a few at a time. He'd warn them about women, chocolate milk shakes, lying in bed too long. He'd tell them what a wonderful day he and I had had, and they'd wink at me knowingly.

I always watched Frank's match if I wasn't wrestling him myself. He moved really well for "a big fat truck driver," and his costume invariably had the desired effect. He'd whirl his gold cape and hang over the top rope so the marks in the front row could get a good look at the hood. He was one of the few guys who wore full tights with knee pads, and the fans would jeer at him for that—as they always jeered the "bad guy." That was Frank's role; but his basic goodness showed through, so the fans booed him because they felt they ought to, not because they wanted to.

In the middle of a match he'd scream at the referee, "Top of the switch! Top of the switch!" Or another favorite, as he sat in a figure-four leg scissors, was a high-pitched *"Ina grate, ina grate!"*

I asked him once what they meant. He didn't know.

And who knows what Jim ("Goon") Henry meant by yelling, *"Arrshga, arrshga,"* when he had his opponent in

Opposite: Danny McShain dripping blood; right: Handsome Johnny Barend

a headlock? The battle cries over the years were incredible. Danny McShain would throw an elbow and bellow, *"Buckachewie!"* at the same time. Handsome Johnny Barend used *"Whoopa!"* a lot, especially when leapfrogging the other guy. Kola Kwariani liked *"Riggy dig, riggy dig!"* For Wee Willie Davis it was *"Sheeesh, sheeesh!"* through clenched teeth, with much spit flying. And Judo Jack Terry featured *"Seewhathesez, seewhathesez!"*

One particular yell—*"Aalou! Aalou!"*—makes me think of the Sheik.

In Detroit, some years after I graduated from Pratt Institute, my two lives—art and wrestling—came together literally. I had done a self-portrait in oil, a two-by-three-foot canvas, showing me staring intently out at the world. Lord Leighton, the ring announcer, asked me to bring the painting for my prematch ringside interview. In his soft British accent Leighton asked where I'd studied painting, then showed the portrait to the TV audience. It was a serious, thoughtful interview. Suddenly out of the dressing room came the Sheik, eyes bugging insanely. *"Aalou! Aalou!"* He threw fire (I never learned how he did that) from his hand at us, grabbed the painting from Leighton, and smashed it over my head. I stood dumbfounded, my real head poking through where my painted head had been.

The fans went wild.

I returned to art school in the fall of 1953 and continued my double life: Renoir, Rubens, and Picasso by day; headlocks, hammerlocks, and flying tackles by night. I started a series of paintings of that night half of my life.

I always had a sketchbook with me. Waiting in the dressing room, I'd do portraits and sketches of the other wrestlers

Magnificent Maurice

Gino Garibaldi

Larry Simon

(which they loved), my pencil finding in their faces lone-
liness, weariness, disappointment, sometimes even fear
where I hadn't seen it before.

The waiting time hung heavy. Being gregarious by nature,
most of the boys were lost when left to their own devices.

Opposite: Donn and Mark; below: more of the boys, waiting

Above: Clyde Steves, the Golden Terror;
left: Sakura with his Buddha gimmick

They would get their trunks on, lace up their shoes, hang up their wrestling jackets near the shower to steam out, tie their valuables into their handkerchiefs (called "pokes"), and then sit on a bench, hands in their laps, until it was time to go to work. I don't remember any of them reading.

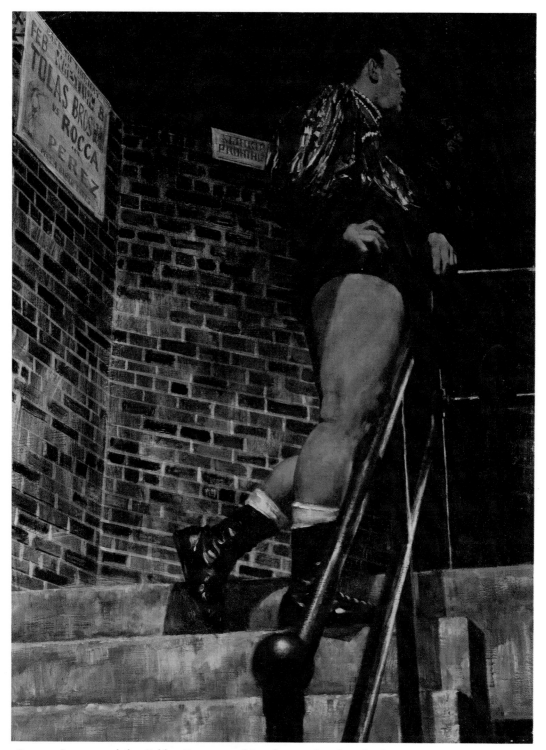

Gregory Jarque and the Golden Terror watching the matches from backstage

Above: Adrian Balargian,
Canadian strongman;
above right: one of the Zebra Kids;
right: Gourdo Chihuahua

Fritz Von Wallack

*Left: Skull Murphy waits
for his match;
below: Sandor Kovacs
with a headlock;
opposite: the Zebra Kids
in the ring*

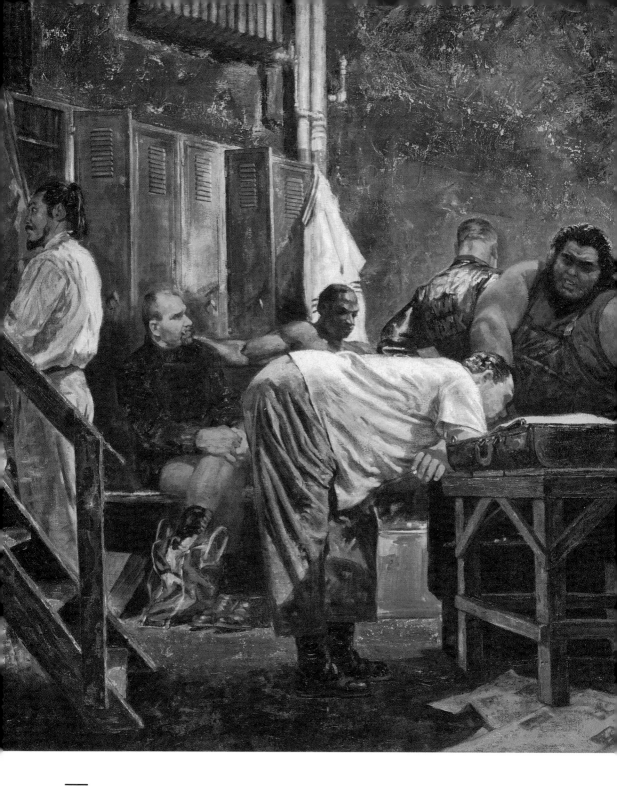

I did several drawings of midget wrestlers: Little Beaver (who sported a Mohawk haircut), Fuzzy Cupid (curly, bleached blond), and Lord Littlebrook. One night Fuzzy had just put on his wrestling gear and was sitting on a bench in the dressing room. He was four feet tall, and when he sat, his feet couldn't reach the floor. He sat with his short arms held straight, knuckles resting on his thighs. My brother Mark happened to be visiting—one of the rare times—and started kibitzing. He had never met Fuzzy, so he went up to him and reached down to shake his hand, saying, "Are you one of the midgets?" Fuzzy laughed and laughed.

And I, dressed for the ring, ready to go on, worked feverishly on a sketch of him, trying to finish it before it was match time for either of us. The other guys watched, fascinated.

Opposite: Haystack Calhoun in the ring, Union City, New Jersey; right: Fuzzy Cupid

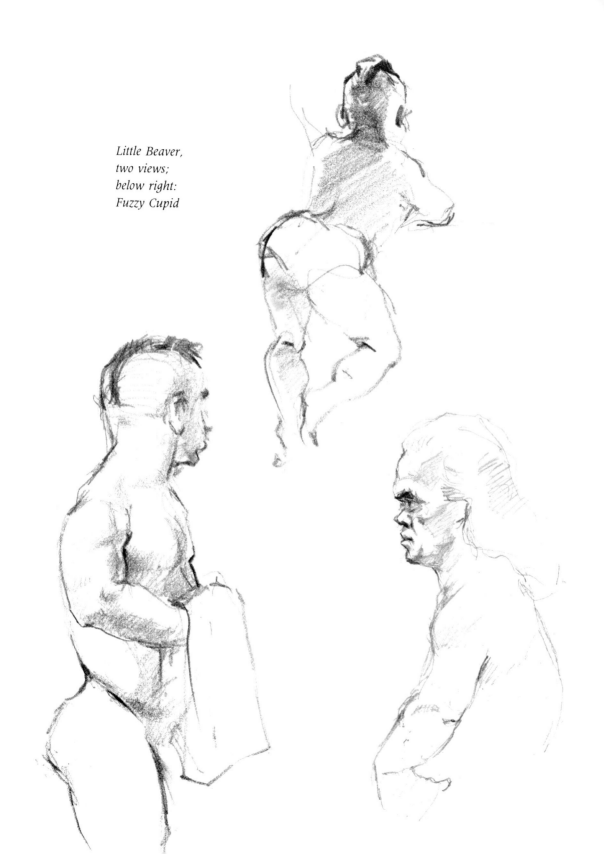

Little Beaver,
two views;
below right:
Fuzzy Cupid

The midgets made the same moves as their full-size counterparts except it took them half as long. One would pick up the other and slam him to the mat in the time a big man needed to get another big man all the way up. During their matches the midgets seemed to be on fast forward, like berserk windup toys. When they got hit, their legs were so short that they'd fall on their ample butts, bounce, and be up so fast you hardly had time to see it.

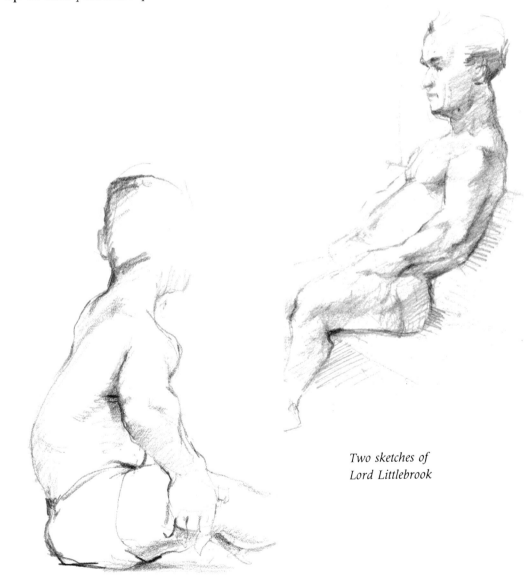

Two sketches of Lord Littlebrook

When they did flying tackles, it was different. It took them what seemed forever to cross that wide expanse of ring and hit the ropes—the bottom two only, of course. A big man could do it in three or four steps.

The crowd never felt the midget wrestlers were getting hurt no matter what they did to one another because they were so small and compact, like children. They had bad backs, broken noses, and cauliflower ears like everyone else—just carried them around in smaller containers.

Injuries

Working five or six nights a week every week of the year—sometimes twice a night—it's only a matter of time before you get hurt. Sprains, brush burns almost to the bone, bruises, pulled muscles, you live with those, but the bad ones you can't live with. I remember one match in the old Madison Square Garden—Dr. Jerry Graham versus Gregory Jarque from Barcelona, Spain. Dr. Jerry weighed three hundred pounds and looked like a Buddha. He could move, but a three-hundred-pound man moves differently from a lighter one. . . .

There wasn't an empty seat in the house, and guys are always up on a night like that—they take chances. Dr. Jerry and Jarque were having a good hot match. The Doctor took Jarque's right arm and whipped him across the ring into the turnbuckle; Jarque hit it with his back and shoulders and bounced off, landing flat on his face on the mat. The Doctor

Dr. Jerry Graham

picked him up again and flung him at the turnbuckle a second time. Jarque hit it hard but grabbed the ropes on either side and held on. Dr. Jerry let out his attack scream and ran like a whirlwind across the ring. He grabbed the top rope with both hands for leverage and vaulted his enormous bulk off the mat into a flying head scissors (a tough move even for a lightweight). He was going really fast. His right leg was supposed to go over Jarque's head, hooking the back of his neck, while the other leg locked his head in. Then the fall, and over Jarque would go.

The Doctor's right leg never got up that far. His knee hit Jarque under the nose and up with the full force of his three hundred pounds. Jarque's nose parted from his face. I never saw so much blood. And Jarque never looked the same.

My time came when I was twenty: a broken leg, which is not supposed to happen. The crack sounded like a pistol shot.

Friday night, Laurel Garden, Newark, New Jersey. It started like dozens of other Friday nights—same fans, same cast of characters.

It was cold and beginning to snow when I arrived. The guy in the outside lobby who was selling wrestling magazines and eight-by-tens of your favorite wrestlers was wrapped up in his scarf like Bob Cratchit from *A Christmas Carol*.

The dressing room was an oven by comparison—big radiator in a small space, plus the body heat of many huge men getting ready to go on. Jack Pfeffer was running around as usual. "You're in the tag match, baby doll!" he said to me as I walked in. According to the printed program, that was the fourth event, so I could take my time lacing up my shoes.

My partner was to be Hal Kanner, an old pal from Brooklyn. We were wrestling another Brooklyn boy, Buddy Gilbert, and Johnny Heidamen.

The dressing room was becoming a steam bath. Finally: "Tag match. Let's go, you're on."

We got started after the usual preliminary instructions and had just begun to gain momentum. I had Johnny Heidamen in a headlock and was pumping it, switching the hold from my left to right arm and back again. He grabbed me around the waist and threw me across the ring. I hit the ropes and flew off. I remember thinking, I'll leapfrog him if he's in the right position. He was in a semicrouch, recovering from the headlock, and in a split second I was upon him.

I reached out to put my hands on his shoulders for the

Opposite: the fall that broke my leg

vault and began my ascent over him when he did something I didn't expect. He stood straight up. I was in midair, my legs spread wide to clear his shoulders, moving forward very fast. I never made it over him. His head caught me full in the groin, knocking the wind out of me and incapacitating me completely. I went straight down in an uncontrolled fall, landing on the inside of my right foot. It snapped out the wrong way; everyone in the hall heard the noise.

The pain was instantaneous, unbearable. The leg started swelling immediately, and my tightly laced wrestling shoes wouldn't allow for it.

I was flat on my back with my right foot at a peculiar angle, looking up at the full moon of the ring light. Then Johnny's, Buddy's, and the referee's heads leaned into the frame of my vision—all staring down at me. The bright lights behind them were diffusing the edges of their silhouettes. It was like being on an operating table.

Johnny Heidamen fell on me as if to pin me and whispered in my ear, "What the hell happened?" I gasped out, "It's broken." He told the ref, and the ref counted to three and raised Johnny's hand when he stood up.

"Faker! Get up, you faker! He never laid a hand on you. Boo! You bum!" screamed the crowd.

They don't understand, I thought. They heard the snap. I'm hurt bad. . . .

Buddy Gilbert knelt down next to me. "I saw what happened."

"It's broken," I said. "Can't stand the shoe—please get it off."

He looked at the foot and said, "I can't. . . . It's too tight. It's blown up like a blimp."

The match was only minutes old when it died—and the crowd was mad. After all, they'd paid their money. "Boo! Let's get the show on the road. Supposed to be two out of three falls. Get that faker on his feet."

Buddy helped me up. My arm was around the back of his neck, and I was standing on my one good foot. The referee came over to help, and they got me down the stairs and out of the ring, out of the square of light into the dark anger of the crowd. "Bum! Faker!" all the way to the dressing rooms. I was being half carried, my right foot dragging.

"Please, somebody get the shoe off. I can't stand it!"

"We're almost there," said Buddy.

The unmistakable outline of Jack Pfeffer was framed in the light of the dressing-room door. He pushed through the big half-naked wrestlers who had come forward to help, like a tiny jockey shoving past the flanks of huge Belgian horses.

He looked at my foot. "What do I do for a tag match now? I got twenty minutes to fill." He shook his wild mane of hair and disappeared.

They laid me down on a bench. "Let the doc in. Watch it."

I looked up at the doctor's serious black face. "Please get the shoe off," I said. He went to his beat-up old leather bag and came back with a pair of surgical scissors. He cut the laces, and the relief was like the air rushing out of a balloon. He splinted the foot and called an ambulance.

The rest of the matches went on after a prolonged intermission. I lay there in that hot box of a dressing room, hurting and sweating. Johnny Heidamen came in from the shower, drying himself with a towel. He was very upset. "I didn't do it," he said.

He looked around at the other guys. "I didn't do it."

I told him, "Don't worry about it. . . . It happens. Not supposed to, but it does. It wasn't your fault."

The matches were long over when the ambulance finally came from the city hospital. I had my trunks and one wrestling shoe on and was still sweating profusely. I put on the short jacket I wore to enter the ring and tossed my street clothes into my wrestling bag. Johnny, along with some other boys, helped me out past the dark ring, past the now empty rows of ringside seats that had been full of people with angry voices, out through the long lobby to the waiting ambulance.

It was snowing steadily then. I snapped up my jacket against the cold. My legs were bare. I began to shiver violently.

The emergency room looked like the terrible Civil War battlefield at Shiloh.

The ambulance attendants wheeled me in on a gurney and helped me onto a chair. Doctors and nurses were hustling past, doing perfunctory examinations, then disappearing for long periods of time. Many of them didn't speak English.

I sat there in my trunks with only one shoe on and bare legs. No one noticed. It was maybe two hours before some orderlies got to me and took me to the X-ray room. After that—a long time later—an Asian doctor came over and pointed at my leg, then at himself. I assumed that meant he was going to set it. I made some gestures to suggest he look at the X rays first. He smiled.

Different orderlies wheeled me upstairs into a treatment room. It was dreary but at least quiet. The doctor looked quizzically at the wrestling shoe, my trunks, and my bare legs, then proceeded to apply the wet gauze for a cast—a very strange-looking cast, as it turned out. It was thick at the top and thin where the break was and required an hour to finish. The doctor smiled, made an ''all through'' gesture, and left. I sat there on the table. It was dead quiet. There was no one around. I waited. It was four o'clock in the morning.

My leg hurt like hell. Funny . . . I thought breaks quit hurting once they were set. At four-thirty I got myself off the table and hobbled over to the door of the treatment room. I looked down the dingy institutional-green corridor. There was no one in sight, so, leaning against the wall with my back and both hands, I began inching along like a spider.

I reached the end and saw my reflection in the glass door there—my red, white, and blue wrestling jacket set off starkly against the green wall, my bare legs, one high-topped shoe, and an oddly twisted cast. I looked through the doors at the maze of corridors ahead of me and felt strangely detached.

By the time I found the elevator and got back to the emergency room, I had completely ruined—by walking on it—what hadn't been much of a cast in the first place. I retrieved my wrestling bag with my street clothes in it, took out a dime, and called friends to come and get me.

Three days later the emergency-room cast was sawed off, the leg reset, and a proper cast applied. It was two months before I started working again.

Riots

Y ou'd think with all the prodding and goading of the fans that riots at matches would have happened often. They didn't, but when they occurred, it was terrible.

The worst place to be was in the ring. The other boys would be standing by the bleachers in the chute to the dressing room in relative safety, but up there, you were exposed.

You could usually tell when some blowup was about to happen. The crowd would be at fever pitch. Then one mark would jump up onto the apron of the ring, sometimes armed with a bottle or knife. He'd get between the ropes and head for his target—whichever of the wrestlers he didn't like (for instance, one much hated "bad guy" was Fritz Von Wallack. His gimmick was wearing a monocle, which he thought made him look the villain; he would punctuate his matches with yells of *"Sieg Heil"* and the stiff-armed Nazi salute. Everyone knew that during the day he was a conductor on the old Myrtle Avenue El train in Brooklyn. But that didn't make any difference: they'd boo him anyway).

So there would be this crazed fan with a weapon. In seconds the two wrestlers in the ring would make hamburger of him. And all hell would break loose.

Rows of steel chairs would be hurled into the ring, bottles, paper clips shot with rubber bands (a real danger for your eyes). The rest of the boys would spill en masse out of the

Fritz Von Wallack gives the Nazi salute.

Von Wallack on the ropes

chute, pulling off their watches and stuffing them into their pockets, shoving their way through the crowd.

In the ring the guys would be punching or grabbing the marks as they came—tossing them aside like clothing dummies. Finally the wedge of wrestlers from the floor would break through and be up on the apron. The unlucky fans were the ones now caught in the ring. They were trespassing on sacred territory, and did they pay the penalty!

Soon the police, referees, and officials would all be in the ring. There'd be a great shove into the masses, with the two principal wrestlers in the center, the whole moving like a giant cell, undulating and squeezing its way toward the safety of the dressing room. There the two principals would split off through the door. The objects of its hatred gone, the crowd would back off and break up, its fury dissipated.

What was supposed to be contained—allowed out gradually over the course of the matches—had popped like a champagne cork. The evening had burst beyond the wrestlers' control, leaving only a sour emptiness.

Asylum

You never knew where a booking would take you. One—when I was twenty-three years old—took four of us to Northport Veterans' Hospital.

There were several buildings, across acres of beautifully manicured lawn, set off by stage-scenery shrubbery and trees. Leading to them was a long gently curving road, which we followed with some feelings of apprehension. There was no evidence of human activity anywhere—just green lawns and great shade trees filtering the bright sunlight.

Bull Curry, who was driving, raised his shoe-brush eyebrow and said, "I wonder if it's the one with the heavy wire screens on the windows?" There was no one to ask. We pulled up to the entrance of the building with the screens. Bull stopped the car.

The building doors opened suddenly and out came a group of white-suited attendants, their uniforms eye shattering in the sunlight. One who seemed to be in charge leaned over and looked into the car at Bull, then at the rest of us.

"You must be the wrestlers. We're waiting for you."

We all got out, opened the trunk, and reached in for our bags. The attendants grinned foolishly at us. All right, some of us looked a little funny: Bull had two enormous cauliflower ears and one black inch-thick continuous eyebrow; Skull Murphy had no hair anywhere—not even his eyebrows; Baron Scicluna, six foot five, from the isle of Malta; and me.

The white-suited man in charge ushered us into the building. We entered a small dark stairwell and waited while he fumbled with an enormous ring of keys. He found the right one and opened the steel door, which had a small wire-and-glass window in it. This opened onto a sun-drenched staircase completely enclosed by heavy wire mesh. As we got to each landing, there was another metal door with a wire-and-glass window, through which you could see a long corridor with doors on either side—but no people. We got to the top floor, and the white-suited man again fumbled with the keys, got the steel door open, and led us out into a corridor. It smelled faintly of urine and sour milk. There was a mop and a pail; someone had just cleaned this section of the ward, and the floor gleamed. Sunlight streamed in everywhere.

"Right in here, fellas. Shower over there. Anything you need, gimme a call." The white-suited man left.

"Gives me the creeps!" said Bull. "Is the wire to keep us from them or them from us?"

We opened our bags and began to get undressed. We

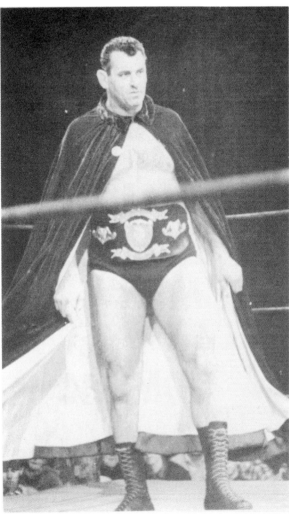

Above right: Bull Curry;
above: Baron Scicluna;
right: Skull Murphy

were talking and lacing up shoes when Skull nudged me with his elbow. I looked up, and in the doorway were some of the residents. They were very old, hollow eyed, and overwhelmingly melancholy. They stood there, backlit by the bright sunny square of light from the door across the hall. They said nothing, just looked.

The attendant came back. "You guys ready?"

"Yeah, in a minute," Skull said. "Are all the . . . ah . . . er . . . inmates that old?"

"Nah! The patients on this floor are. We got some kids from the Korean War, too. These guys are World War One mostly." (I thought of Sid riding backward on that mule.)

Dressed now for the ring, we followed the attendant down the hall to the stairwell again. Sad faces now faded in and out of doorways.

There were some men in doctors' uniforms waiting to greet us in a large room on the ground floor. We looked into an adjacent auditorium with rows of empty chairs and a ring set up in the middle. "Welcome, gentlemen. Thanks for coming," said one of the doctors. "The men will be down in a minute. . . . Ah, there they come now."

Down either side of the auditorium they filed, led by white-suited, key-laden attendants. Ancient men, young men—some not much more than teenagers. In an almost military fashion they shuffled into row after row and filled the hall. The whole procedure was silent. When they were all seated, we jogged down one aisle.

Bull Curry stopped at the apron, picked out one "fan," and began his screaming harangue, which, coupled with his eyebrow, usually brought a crowd to its feet. Silence—

except for Bull's own insane screaming. The old man he'd addressed was far away, in some long-ago battle now all his own. Bull paused, looked over at the rest of us, then joined us in the ring. The bell rang, and our strange tag match began. The only sounds were our own voices yelling at one another, the sounds of our bodies hitting the mat, and our own grunts and groans.

"Listen to us!" I whispered to Scicluna. "There's usually so much noise from the crowd you can't hear yourself. This is weird."

We did all the things calculated to turn a regular audience into a yelling, screaming mass. . . . Silence.

The doctors and attendants smiled and seemed to be enjoying themselves. . . . Then there was a loud, unintelligible scream from the front row. One middle-aged patient was on his feet, shouting, his eyes open, seeing nothing. An attendant rushed to him, tried to quiet him, and finally took him away. His display seemed to upset the man next to him, who was sitting with his back to the ring. He yelled, "Outlaws!" over and over. Then, finally, he slipped again into quiet reverie.

We tried to penetrate their private places but failed miserably. The match came to an end.

The men filed out as they had filed in. We left the ring shaken by our inability to reach them. It had never happened to any of us before. We followed our attendant back up the wire-screened stairwell.

"Why do you have the matches?" I asked.

He smiled cheerfully. "It's the one thing in here they all like."

Al Ravenna, *World Telegram & Sun*

Mark, me, and Donn

School's Out

Thank God for the wrestling. All those hours spent painting sample pictures, paying calls on publishers with my portfolio, waiting for the phone to ring . . . it was hard keeping body and soul together. The three or four bookings a week were keeping me alive: Washington, Baltimore, Bridgeport, Hartford, Pittsburgh, and, mercifully, sometimes closer to home—Rollerama or Sunnyside Gardens.

For a while there were almost as many wrestlers as art students in the neighborhood around Pratt Institute. Even Mark and Donn showed up for part of 1959, and sometimes we were booked for six-man tag matches.

My brothers took a room in an old Victorian mansion-turned-rooming-house three blocks from my apartment. It was a great old house built around a central hall. At the end of the hall was a magnificent curving mahogany staircase with a single-seat elevator attached next to the wall. The rich old lady who had owned the house became crippled and had the contraption installed. The dozens of rooms were filled with art students—and Mark and Donn. It wasn't long before they were joined by Dangerous Danny McShain and Handsome Johnny Barend. Wrestlers tend to flock.

While I had painting and my future career to focus on, they would spend the day prowling the neighborhood with nothing to do until we all left for the evening's matches.

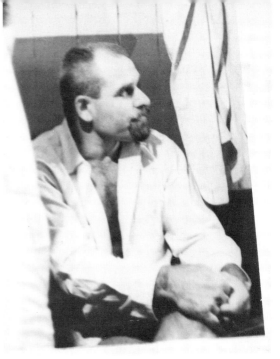

The photos on this and the three following pages are references I used to paint the dressing room panorama reproduced in color on pages 94–95.

Mark decided he'd start painting "to express himself." I gave him a big canvas and some oil paints. After a bit he asked me to come see the canvas. His room was a clutter of open wrestling bags, shoes, and drying gear. Hung over the back of a chair were the rubber cables he worked out with. On another chair his canvas was propped up. It was terrible. At the bottom was a smear of bright yellow paint, slowly turning to orange. At the top, fiery red. I said with a straight face, "Very interesting. What does it mean?" He said, "In the yellow area I'm calm. Then in the orange area, I'm getting mad." Finally pointing at the red area, he said, "Now I'm *really* mad." I nodded knowingly. He was so serious.

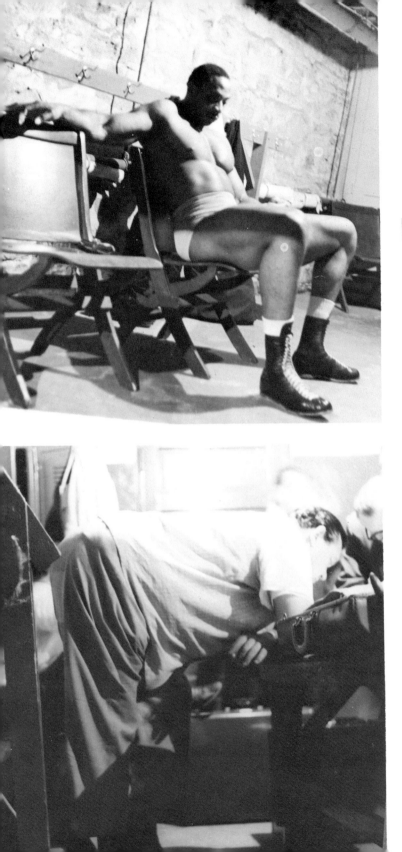

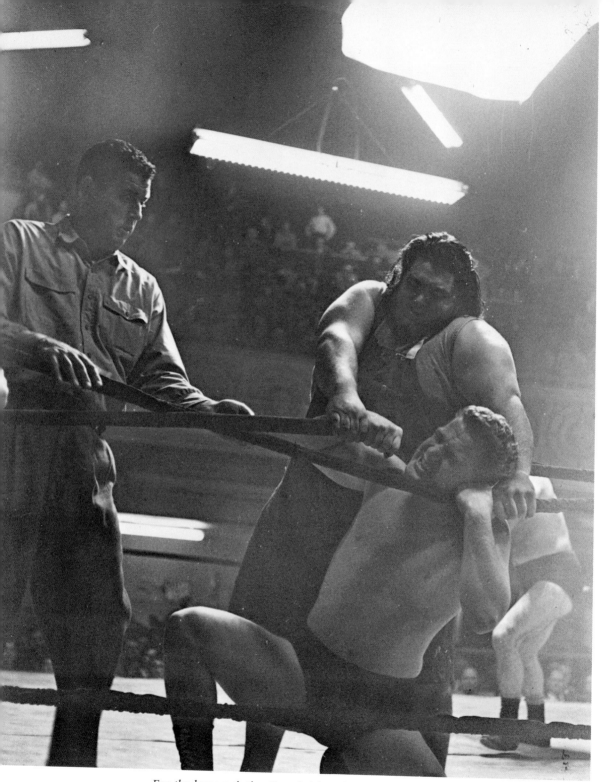

For the large painting I used this action shot of Haystack Calhoun in
the ring but changed the setting and eliminated his partner.

Left: Mark and Donn pose for me; above: photo of Harry Lewis used for reference

Mark was a great mimic—he caught exactly the way Danny McShain would snap the elastic of his Jockey shorts with his thumb—but painting was not for him.

I started doing illustrations for men's pulp magazines. Sex, violence, war. Not much money, but work—a start.

The wrestlers would say, "How's it going? What magazine will it be in? I want to get a copy." They were proud

of me. I came into the dressing room one night, and Dr. Jerry Graham exclaimed, ''I saw it!'' almost swallowing his big cigar.

I said, ''Saw what?''

''I was sitting on a train,'' he said, ''and I opened up this magazine I bought, and there was a story about spies and Nazis. The illustration showed a guy on the ground, an SS man holding him down with a perfect double wristlock. I thought, That's got to be one of Ted's illustrations. And sure enough, there was your name in the corner: illustrated by Ted Lewin. I just knew, because that wristlock was perfect.''

Opposite: me signing an autograph for a fan; below: the magazine illustration

Epilogue

Donn retired to Honolulu, where he pumps iron five hours a day and recently placed third in the Mr. Hawaiian Islands Bodybuilding Contest, beating out many twenty-year-olds.

Mark still travels all over the world and remains a disembodied voice on the phone in the middle of the night.

Sallee lives in Houston, Texas, and raises miniature pinschers. She stayed married to Dangerous Danny, who, because of his wrestling injuries, had both hips replaced. He was still dangerous, but with a cane, until the day he died.

And I married my wife, Betsy, in 1963. We met at Pratt and live in Brooklyn not far from the school.

Opposite: ''The winner!''—Laurel Garden

Glossary

WRESTLING LINGO

Apron   Edge of the ring

The book   A record of bookings

Card   A program of wrestling matches

Cauliflower ears   Puffy ears from repeated injuries

Corner post   The ring ropes are suspended from the four corner posts by the use of turnbuckles.

Crack wise   Make sarcastic remarks about the business

Draw   Time limit reached, no winner

Elbow smash   Hitting an opponent with the front of the forearm and elbow, which is legal, as opposed to punching with the fist

Gimmick   A particular mode of dress, persona, or object to rile a crowd

Greenhorn   Beginner

Holds   Various maneuvers employed to subdue an opponent

House   Arena, ballpark, etc., where the matches are held

Lats   The latissimi dorsi muscles

Leapfrogging   Jumping over an opponent's head while he's running at you—as in a flying tackle

Locked horns   Two wrestlers in stances coming together head-on

Mark   A gullible fan

On the card   Being on the program

The pin   A win

Pinned   When a wrestler's shoulders are held to the mat for a count of three

Selling out   No seats left in the house

Shot   A booking

Splash   To fall to the mat, hitting it hard with the arms

Spot show   A special event—not weekly

Stance   Assuming a position ready for action, as in boxing. See photo, page 37.

Sundayed   Hit from the blind side

Territory   Area under the control of one promoter

Turnbuckle   A screw device for putting tension on ropes; covered with a soft, padded fabric in wrestling rings

WRESTLING HOLDS

Arm drag   Take opponent's left arm over your left shoulder and across your chest. Bend over, using arm as a lever, and throw him over your back.

Back drop   Bend over, grab opponent by front of thighs, head between his legs, and stand up quickly, pushing up on his thighs and flipping him over your back. Sometimes done to counter a flying tackle.

Body slam   Face opponent. Put your arm between his legs up to your elbow. Grab him behind the neck with other arm and lift him up and over, slamming him onto the mat.

Cradle   Opponent is lying on his back. Stand over him, take his ankles under your arms, step over his legs, turning him onto his stomach. Sit back. Usually a submission hold.

Dropkick   Leap into the air, bringing your body parallel to the ring mat, knees bent. Shoot both feet forward, hitting your opponent in the head or neck area. Land with a "splash." See left photo, page 13.

Double wristlock   Grasp opponent's left wrist with your right hand. Place your left arm in the bend of his arm and grasp your own right wrist.

Figure-four leg scissors   Put left leg around opponent with your left foot hooked under your right knee, making a figure H.

Flying head scissors   See page 101.

Flying mare   Take your opponent by the back of his head and throw him over your shoulder. See right photo, page 13.

Flying tackle   Bounce off the ropes for momentum, run across the ring, and knock your opponent down with your shoulder.

Front face lock   Take opponent's head under your left arm. Place your right arm under his left arm. Quickly sit down while lifting opponent up and over onto his back.

Go-behind   Various moves to get behind your opponent in preparation for a takedown

Hammerlock   Bend opponent's arm behind his back and push it up toward opponent's head. Sometimes done in conjunction with a double wristlock.

Headlock   See photo, page 45.

Hip throw   Hook opponent under his arm and behind his head and pull him over your hip. Can also be done from a headlock.

Knee lift   Get opponent in front face lock. Swing right knee back and up, then swing it forward and up quickly, into your opponent's head and neck. See photo, page 51.

Rowboat   See pages 44–46.

Takedown   Various moves to put your opponent on the mat, such as an arm drag or a front face lock

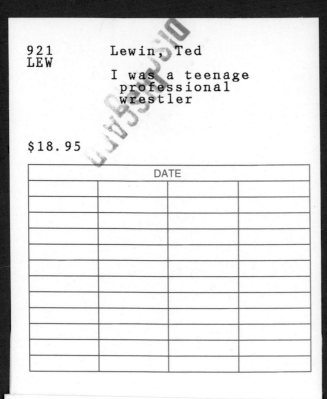

921
LEW

Lewin, Ted

I was a teenage
professional
wrestler

$18.95

DATE			

BAKER & TAYLOR